PIRATES NEVER
TAKE TURNS!

PIRATES NEVER TAKE TURNS!

Written by
KEN GAGNE

Illustrated by
SARA KUBA

For Aubree

IN a *cold* and *creepy*
Haunted house
On the corner of Spooky & Fright...

A ghoulish gang of MONSTERS loomed
And *lurked*
On Halloween night.

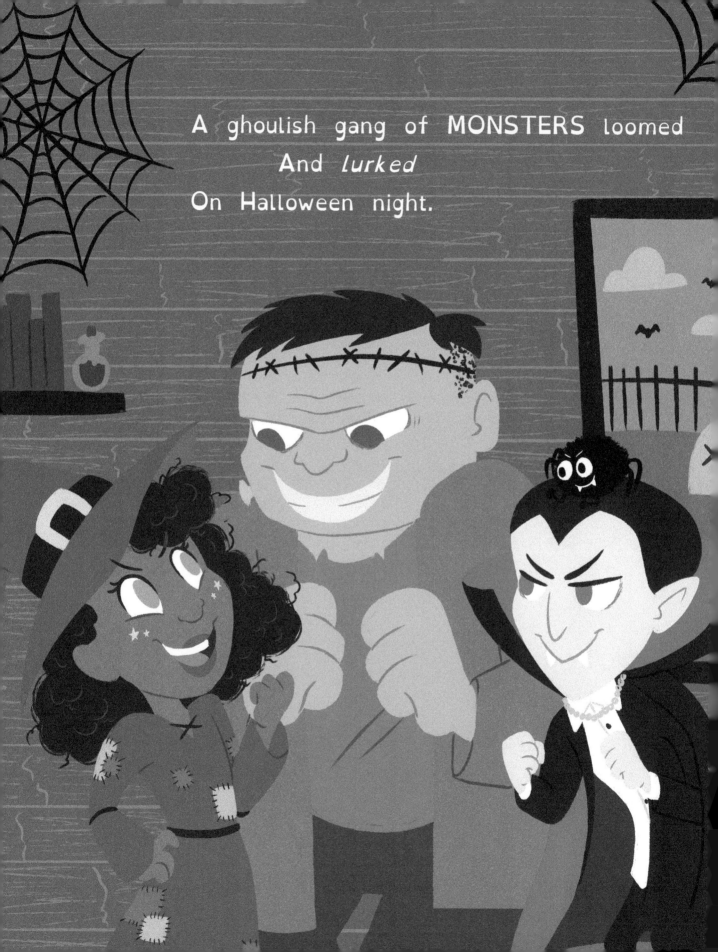

Their **PLAN**: the same as *every* year...
When trick-or-treaters came by,
The fiendish friends would *all take turns*
To **TAUNT** and **TERRIFY**!

But when they heard a *knockety-knock*,
They opened the door and revealed...
     A horrible, horrid, deplorable PIRATE.
        "BLIMEY!" the monsters squealed.

Patch on her eye and hook on her hand,
     The brute buccaneer did *BOOM*,
"Arrrgh! Make way for CAPTAIN CUTLASS,
Or else meet yer *DOOM!*"

A menacing sword hung low on her belt;
The color of *night* was her hat.
"*By thunder!* Me here to scarify kids!
And THAT," she blurted, "is THAT!"

"Yes, please join us," Dracula said.
"Be our guest,
Go first,
Let's see...
After you will come Witchy then Frankenstein,
And last, but not least, will be me."

Cutlass agreed with a *grim, greedy grin,*
And the ghastly group ducked by the door.
    THEN...
Just as a trickle of toddlers arrived,
The pirate **LEAPED OUT** with a *ROAR!*

"Avast, ye scurvy scallywags!
RETREAT in the *blink* of an eye!
OR... walk the plank and sink-sunk-sank,
For Captain Cutlass AM I!"

The terrorized tots *took off* like a shot,
And the monsters were mighty impressed!
    In fact, they applauded the lauded marauder,
Who *clearly* had prepped for the test.

Up next,
The witch grabbed hold of her broom
When a shabby sheep peeped, "Trick or Treat!"
BUT... Cutlass swung out of the sky *on a vine*
And KNOCKED Witchy off of her feet!

"Back to yer cauldron, warty old toad!
 Make haste!
Let the Captain on through!"
 THEN
The petulant pirate reviled the child
And *guzzled* the Halloween brew!

Frankenstein staggered and stomped toward the door
When *his* turn to scare came around...
BUT
Cutlass burst out of a brambly bush
And forced **FRAZZLED** Frank to the ground!

"OUTTA me sight, ye bucket of bolts!
Away with ye now! *Double quick!*
For none but pirates are right prepared
To properly TREAT or TRICK!"

Dracula turned himself into a bat
And *frantically* flew out in front.
　　But... Cutlass rejected that **BAT** with her **HAT**
And *shooed him away* with a grunt!

She snagged **ALL** the bags from the *mystified* mites
And kept it up **ALL** the night long!
Then, after she chased away every last tyke,
She shouted a sinister song...

There ain't no monster, ghoul, or goblin
Near as MEAN as ME!
And if ye try to prove yerself
I'll TOSS ye in the sea,
Where gators SNAP and sharks ATTACK,
As every swabbie learns!
OHH! Yo-Ho-Ho and Shiver Me Timbers...

Now... what happened NEXT,
　　(Legend alleges),
When Cutlass concluded that ditty,
Her plucky pet parrot, Polly Roger,
Delivered the *nitty* and *gritty*...

Feathers aflutter,
He uttered the words
That *SHOOK* the invader with fear...
　　　　"SQUAWK! Better *behave*, or Shanty Claus
　　　　　　　Won't give you goodies this year!"

WELL...
A frown found her face, 'cause pirates, you see,
Want "Shanty" to visit them *too.*
Yet, many require reminders
To ditch doing devious deeds that they do.

"**ALAS**, me hearties, yer pardon me begs,"
The seadog said, chin on her chest.

"Ye landlubbers welcomed a swashbuckling bucko. At BEST, me a PEST of a GUEST."

SO...

As Cutlass unloaded the booty she pillaged,
(No one's quite sure the amount),
She apologized *over* and *over* again
                    To Witchy,
            Frank,
                    And the Count.

BUT...
Before the Captain boarded her "ship"
To cruise off into the night,
She BOOGIED back up to that haunted house...

And hugged those monsters tight!

The grateful *mates* all waved goodbye,
Agreeing that NEXT Halloween,
They'd treat every kid to a *treasure* of sweets...

And *take turns* NOT being mean!

ABOUT THE AUTHOR

Ken Gagne is not a pirate or a monster, and he has **NEVER** cut anyone in line. He did not invent writing, nor has he penned one thousand best-selling novels (yet). Ken does not routinely refer to himself in the third person. Proud parents of two grown humans, he and his wife live in New Jersey with their cat, Gary—who coincidentally used to be a pirate in one of his eight previous lives. Unless he's hiding under his bed with them, you can find Ken Gagne and his books at a top-secret location, cryptically dubbed www.kengagnebooks.com by an expert team of highly trained domain-namers. Please buy Ken's books; he owes bad people money.

ABOUT THE ILLUSTRATOR

Sara Kuba secretly believes her sketchbook is an enchanted portal to the Land of Doodles. Armed with an unofficial "Drawing Adorable Stuff" degree from Ringling College of Art and Design (way more prestigious than it sounds), she specializes in creating characters and children's illustrations that are cute enough to make teddy bears jealous. When she's not drawing, Sara moonlights as a professional cat-wrangler and occasionally bakes cookies for her imaginary friends. In her spare time, which is hardly ever (not really), she enjoys juggling flaming bowling pins and decoding the secrets of the universe. You can reach her (if you're tall enough) at www.artofskuba.com.

Printed in the USA
CPSIA information can be obtained
at www.ICGtesting.com
LVHW072149301023
762625LV00009B/52